# WIND, TREES

# Wind, Trees

JOHN FREEMAN

Copper Canyon Press
Port Townsend, Washington

Cover art: Piet Mondrian, *Tree*, 1912.
Photograph copyright Bildarchiv Foto Marburg / Art Resource, NY

Copper Canyon Press is in residence at Fort Worden State Park
in Port Townsend, Washington, under the auspices of Centrum.
Centrum is a gathering place for artists and creative thinkers from
around the world, students of all ages and backgrounds,
and audiences seeking extraordinary cultural enrichment.

LIBRARY OF CONGRESS CATALOGING-IN-PUBLICATION DATA
Names: Freeman, John, 1974- author.
Title: Wind, trees / John Freeman.
Description: Port Townsend, Washington : Copper Canyon Press, 2022.
  | Summary: "A collection of poems written by John  Freeman"
  — Provided by publisher.
Identifiers: LCCN 2022019503 (print) | LCCN 2022019504 (ebook)
  | ISBN 9781556596483 (trade paperback)
  | ISBN 9781619322660 (epub)
Subjects: LCGFT: Poetry.
Classification: LCC PS3606.R445465 W56 2022  (print)
  | LCC PS3606.R445465 (ebook) | DDC 811/.6—dc23/eng/20220422
LC record available at https://lccn.loc.gov/2022019503
LC ebook record available at https://lccn.loc.gov/2022019504

98765432 FIRST PRINTING

COPPER CANYON PRESS
Post Office Box 271
Port Townsend, Washington 98368
www.coppercanyonpress.org

*for Martha*

We are a shape the wind makes in these leaves
as it passes through. We are not the wood
any more than the fire, but the heat which is a marriage
between the two.

Jack Gilbert, "Music Is in the Piano
Only When It Is Played"

# Contents

Sleeping in the Cross Breeze   3

## WIND

Decoys   7

Boxing   8

Loneliness   11

Perfume   12

Dawn in Erie, Pennsylvania   13

Wind   14

Helping   15

Friendship   16

Perigee   17

Passing   18

Take It   19

Nothing to Declare   21

Ending   22

Rain   24

The Commute   25

Piano   26

Signs   27

Saturday   29

Night Train    30

The Heat Is Coming    31

Windward    33

Yard Dogs    34

Dream    35

Burning the Days    36

Sailing    37

Quarantine    38

Airless    39


TREES

Shipbuilding    43

Singing    45

The Language of Trees    46

Wood    49

Among the Trees    50

Still    51

Show    52

The Secret Country    53

Borrowed Finery    54

Icicle    57

Centuries in the Woods    58

Exile    59

The Trees of City Hall    61

Windbreak    63

Dusk    64

Colors    65

Receiving    68

Without    69

The Green Tram    70

Fables   72

The Red Umbrella   73

Voices   75


*Acknowledgments*   79

*About the Author*   81

# WIND, TREES

# Sleeping in the Cross Breeze

The air's sweet tonight
across the sheets
your hair a tidal wash
what boat is this
why does the sea feel
so calm some evenings
so dark on others
what is love but feeling
there's no compass
no wind no destination
just air this breeze
blue as night your
body by moonlight

# Wind

# Decoys

Bomber pilots knew wind could be a mercy seven thousand feet up
river like a pelican's neck  engine drone a chorus of song
clouds could be a mercy rain could be a mercy snow could be
a mercy  the wrong type of moon

did ties whistle and whip when a payload was cut began
its nearly eight-minute journey back to Earth the silence
of that descent frightening to them sitting in the sky goggled
and scarfed delivering death like a baby from above

who thought to name a thirteen-foot-long four thousand-pound
bomb Satan  had that person ever crouched close as a plane birthed
a payload that drifted  did he wonder about the free will of objects
we set in motion how they resist us as if a silent hand

sometimes saying no  during World War I when
the Germans were using zeppelins in aerial campaigns
the French planned to build a fake Paris fifteen miles north
on the river complete with a replica street plan Arc de Triomphe

working trains snuffed-out lights that at night
might fool the bombers who'd fly right over a blacked-out Paris
engine drones a lullaby they never had to use
the war ended in 1918 all vestiges of the city outside the city

destroyed  Fernand Jacopozzi the engineer who'd designed
the stage-set Paris lit the Eiffel Tower instead
then died in his home in 1932 at age fifty-four his lasting gift
the realization that good and evil are both drawn to light

# Boxing

In the waning days
of those years in London
I took up boxing. I didn't
want to unload on some
unsuspecting soul so I
found a sparring partner.
She turned up, neck
tatted, face pierced, dread-
locked and strong as hell.
A Turkish woman with
*East London* stenciled
on her left forearm. Before
boxing she trained horses
in dressage and before
that was trying not to
drown herself in drink.
After an hour I was losing
my breakfast and last night's
dinner. See you Wednesday
she said not discussing
whether there'd be an *if.* Thus
my living room turned into a
boxing gym. Couch the cut
corner. Not once did she knock
me down, but she could have.
I did that all on my own, using
my shoulder for the cross
rather than my hips, leaping
at the uppercut. Thinking it was
about power rather than grace.
I'd done this before, retreated from what
couldn't be controlled by measuring

rage out in iron. One plate, two,
the stack. The infernal
music you play in a room
that's mostly rubber and steel.
Thinking if I were just strong enough in my
body I could carry it all.
Making a racket. Skipping
rope. Meantime Dad's at home
losing hope. Some muscles you
don't make out of joy.
Then Carla shows up in her
car fumed in weed. Horse-
hair still on her hands. Like this,
she'd say, and stop a hook
right below my eye. Glove sweat
and wrap funk. Rope slap, foot
squeak, cut time, then out
on the roads. Flesh tumbled
from my body. My lungs
endless. I stopped hitting something
and poured my body into a form.
At my desk my feet moving. I began
running before we'd spar. What, I don't
work you hard enough? she said once,
catching me outside, still sweaty
in my trainers, then ran
me until I puked. What do you
want, she asked. Are you here
to hurt someone? We can do
that. I didn't need to answer, I was
there to accept the world was
going to punch. To remember

it may not mean harm
but that's precisely why I needed
to be ready for when it would.

We took to boxing on the roof.
The noise had woken a neighbor
who complained down the mews,
so the last spring, as the sky lost
the color of a bruise and daylight
arrived earlier, we set up
under the blue ceiling
of the world and threw hooks and
combinations, breath
drowning out traffic on the avenue.
I'd learned by then most power
came from my ass. But I'd forget.
Throw with my arm. A chill
spring morning I was hitting
one two, one two three, and a
voice comes over the wind
light as a falling leaf—
*nah mate, just flick it, like this*
and we both look up.
There's a builder across the
way, footwork loose, dancing
on the scaffolding he's
tethered to, floating
nonetheless, arms faster than
air. *Like this.*

# Loneliness

Sundays I'd walk down the hill toward the green, four o'clock
    dark beginning like a rumor—
always she was leaning over the counter, head tipped toward
    a tiny phone,
her husband turning the pages of a
*Daily Mail* like a man
      whose suspicions of human nature were
      being fed fresh evidence.
Stale fryer fat, ale, black and tans in the fridge.
They knew I'd be there before the match started.
*You alright yeah*
Every Sunday a matinee I attended for three years
as volcanoes exploded
and she died,
white slipped into my beard,
wars began and others ended.
Each Sunday the words gathering new weight
strangeness
as words do when you repeat them.
*You alright*
I didn't know but by halftime if I wasn't too pissed
I'd walk home in the furred darkness before the beer wore off
and a sudden gust of wind could blow cold air on my heart.

# Perfume

I woke to the memory
of walking up Barbès
holding hands with you
our feet guiding us toward
the market. Eyes on
tomatoes and cherries
Tunisian desserts
huge piles of garlic.
The onion touts
hoarse at ten a.m.
from shouting.
The tangerine seller
undressing one
fruit after the other
misting the air.

# Dawn in Erie, Pennsylvania

A church, Shaker,
at the base of a
roadway sloped and
bald, last week's
salt has drawn all the
secret water from
the asphalt. Street
empty, blue
and black and quiet.
A Mobil station
at the end of the
block, a glowing sign:
Gas $2.80 a gallon.

# Wind

The gods sent wind from the sea
to cool senators' heat
seduce agitators from politics into
their lovers' beds
or in the case of Zephyrus
transport Psyche to Eros's abode
as faithfully as an island ferry

Now we know wind is a gap
in atmospheric pressure
gases flowing from high to low
so leaves turn up their tips
umbrellas bend back and roofs
rip off maybe a small cross breeze
blows sweat off our burning bodies

Lights out on an August night
in a noisy city windows open fans
turning minds afire with the world
It's all high pressure now
slamming against itself
in the upper air

How we long for that eye
watching us from a cave in Thrace
saying  pause here friend
we all need wind
and water  heart's ease

# Helping

In summer fires
singed so much
of the valley
ranchers brought
goats to the freeway verge
and set them loose
to rip brush
and chomp foliage
do whatever goats
get up to on hillsides. None
of them clambered
down to the roadway.
Instead they followed
wind just as fire does
climbing up and up
the sky so dry it could
cut your skin. Driving
by on the highway you
could spot them—a
dozen or so solemn
unheroic firefighters
daubs of white in a
field of heavy smoke—
bringing the tiniest
bit of balance to
those tanned rolling
hills of flame. Reach
down to adjust the air-
conditioning and you'd
miss them completely.

# Friendship

Woken in the blue hours, starlings dive and swirl
in the dark. I grind coffee, carry it to the garden,
count the hours back to you. Too many and too
few. Summers you'd retreat to the den
for August baseball, the mature cedar and
Douglas fir darkening to deep shade at dusk.
Night games and their holy liturgy. Windups
and changeups, the living box score. Base
hits and pine tar, inside heat and extra innings.
Now I worry you're keeping vigil over the smoking
tree line. Knowing when the roar of fire gets close
it's time to go. Decades those trees kept counsel,
told you when wind was coming, or snow. I like
to think on stark forest nights when you were alone,
you were not alone, that they brought news of
bear cubs, of what newts cared to say,
how a dream could grow in the gap between
the forest floor and the first run of branches,
make of a river and its brambles a home, if you
learned to live without taking alone. So many offerings
are new requests. A mistake I nearly made that cold
fall. We'd finished our walk and tuned in to the
Yankees game, I wanted to reach out, grab
your hand so you knew my gratitude, instead I heard
a voice in the warm inner air. It said, Relax, we're
speaking by simply sitting here.

# Perigee

On nights when the moon
is like a hand on my cheek
and the gentler darkness
says this one is done
you've made it
In the morning there may
be the sharp whiff of coffee
or a breeze that carries
the curtains in or an arm
over your body you must
lift to get up as if the weight
of the world can be measured
in small gestures
On these nights my gratitude
reaches its perigee and I
close my eyes     try not
to feel the moment I begin
falling again     falling back into
the outer darkness

# Passing

Walking to a pool hall we
pass down an empty street
late summer shutters open
light brushes the top of my
head I look up and meet
a woman's eyes staring
down from a third-floor
window   She wears a
a thin black party dress
behind her a chandelier
glows   It's early evening
the night could go another
way and for the length
of a stride it could

## Take It

For months we learned the new ways
we were to die or not to die to avoid

dying to almost die and feel lucky
for not dying but strange because there

was a lightness in the head afterward
as if something essential had been

removed—and then one day constables arrived
in twos to tell us that our homes were not

our homes we needed to go it seemed
to happen overnight these men with polished boots

who had given them so much white paper, so much
up-to-date information they were merely the waterfall

at rivers' ends they had children themselves what
would happen if they didn't follow the law this cloud

cover, this rule like gravity as the hospitals began
to fill banks hadn't sent notes to monkish clerks

typing in their cells a name, amount, address, number
of months behind notice number final warning

phonecallattempteddepositclaimed value of rent lost
as if lawyers hadn't driven into work masked and cleansed

to polish motions that they'd give to associates
to slide through clogged courts,

as if paralegals hadn't stayed up late drinking
coffee in paper cups writing down names, surely some of them

aware, no, that a resident born in 1941 was seventy-nine years old
and would need help packing her things, or maybe she would simply

sit and watch her life carried
to the grass or parking lot the silence after signature

the quiet of forfeiture, *I have done this, I have forfeited what*

*was never mine,* while across town ambulances
move slowly, the heat, and more constables knock

on more doors, and more paralegals stand by more copiers
and more court clerks clack their keys mutely, and more

real-estate trust officers examine their desktops, unhappy
with the CAP rate presented to someone, surely

it's someone, no, a person, yes, a person sitting
in a chair, maybe, could it be a bench, is it in a park,

has he just finished a jog, is he looking at digits
on his phone, thinking, *that's not enough,* as this

person surely it's a person gets in his car
and drives home singing to the radio.

# Nothing to Declare

I stand before it
All that I own
What kind of heaven
would it be if I
couldn't take you

# Ending

Did it come on the night air
like cordite    & ashes

did it move us
to our knees    did we say no

you first please did
we shove the old & then
the lonely the soft
& uncomplaining
to the front

all the slow bodied

anyone cringing
                did we listen to
what was happening
did we deny
did we secret
jewelry while we
waited did we
learn to do it

frightened when it was
clear we already knew how

did we startle at the taste of blood
did we think blood-
lust was simply a word

did we feel our lips

curl back over our teeth
did we find drops of it
        on our faceplates

on our cuff links

after work
scrubbing did it stain
did we weep did we eat
more than ever did it
sharpen our hunger

the keening the animal

wheedling did we remember
how some pleaded did
we bend down & pet them

say this is for the best did they

shake did some take our hands
say    you were my young
you were my children you

were meant to hold me

close did we explain
        there was not enough
did we find once it
started justifications grew
with greed like vines
up the side of a tree
taking everything

# Rain

In the courtyard, a man
puts down his shovel
with a clink. We wait now
as the air cools and mist
begins kissing the limestone
walls, windowsills—the hairs
of our arms. I can almost hear
a melody, but it's coming
from outside. Leaves silver
in the breeze, doves
cease their bickering. Finally,
air rushes into the darkened
apartment, drapes shift, and then
the rain, a theater's curtain drawn.

# The Commute

At the intersection
near Odeon
a man on a red
bicycle straddling
the hot black
pavement leans
forward and shakes
out his long blond
hair. It's not good
hair, its undersides
the color of river
slurry, tips a yellow not made
by nature. But morning
light catches it
as he tosses
the remaining wet
of his recent shower
to the street, flings his
head back and gazes up
at the sun, like an '80s
rock god just before
bursting into a guitar
solo. Crosstown traffic
slows, then stops, and he
pedals off, leaving a damp
halo behind, some
of the light.

# Piano

Who thought to thread
wire through the belly
of a tree, dress its grin with
ivory? Recline it on
its side like a body. Toes to
touch, see. Brilliant blanc,
gold as honey, black as
night lake, it's always wet.
We're all water poured into
form. The mystery
of our making, made in every
thing we make, even
if we have to learn how to play.

# Signs

And I was walking home from the New
       School and at the corner of Eleventh

bent over in pain, like I'd taken a jab to
       the gut following a hard

cross. The next day I hear my
       father's father died of

an internal hemorrhage. I open my phone
       in the Village one morning, my grandmother

asking me for the good news. The next day I
       get the bad news.

And then my phone stopped working
       the month my mother stopped

speaking. All this is on my mind today
       when I see your car in Saint-Germain, not

the one you sold last week, when you
       couldn't walk anymore, but the one

you drove in 1963, when it was new,
       when you were stationed in Germany.

The 250 SL, a white convertible,
       outside Le Bonaparte. If you were in Paris,

this is where we'd go. Who cares if Sartre abandoned
       ship long ago, if Baldwin,

whom you once drank with in the Village, spent more
        time in Turkey than at these marble

tables with their tiny glasses of water and
        swirling waiters. You drove the 250 across

Germany, from the base in Mannheim into prefall
        Prague, your brother squished

into the side seat like a human cartoon. Like your father
        shipping his Cadillac home to

Germany to go on the grand tour, you'd put it
        on a boat, only in the opposite direction,

back home to New Hampshire, where the car ran for years,
        until you began the family and the

business and had the daughter who brought you to me,
        a Californian without a car and missing a

father, tied up in the business of death. I stop in the middle
        of Saint-Germain when I see the Mercedes

this morning. I know that once I cross to the other side of
        the street and sit down, I'm going

to want to take out my telephone
        and call you, to know what I already know.

# Saturday

Wind breaks the afternoon's fermata. A rustle
across the vines

as it blows then stops, a swelling like cheers
if the breeze is sustained.

When the air moves fast, it sounds like rain,
sometimes it is,

other gusts fool the birds who leave and
return with murmurs

of annoyance at false alarms. Until the real thing
makes them go silent.

# Night Train

On the night train to Cleveland elder couples
play cards in twos, Amish boys lurk in the shadows

of their hats, while the rest doze amid
the sweet-potato scent of bodies asleep in numbers.

I tiptoe back to my berth, its itchy starched sheets
and foot-operated sink, its greasy flashing mirror, wishing

you were here to curl up beneath the flicker of passing casino
lights, to do the things we call love when it's night.

# The Heat Is Coming

The heat is coming. An oven door opened in
Damascus in Ankara in Cape Town in Kingston,
gusts of air bring the boiling swelter north.
Now torrid times begin. It doesn't matter,
we don't get to choose our altar. Meteorologists in America
crow over record weather: 117, 118, 122. Not
for a century has the mercury raced
with such alacrity into the red zone.
The ocean is dying but we're dying of
thirst, the power grid over Paris just burst,
they think it's hackers from Novosibirsk

meddling with our thermostats and our elections.

The heat is coming, the cry goes up across
the continent, borders fray and rend, nations
race to break their covenants with each other.
Step away from my breeze, I'll bring you to your knees,
ignore the death of bees, just give us our
daily cake. He said what to whom what a liar
what a cheat it's not strange for flowers to bloom in
December, did you see his latest tweet?

The pavement dries up and dies, that sun will
damage your eyes, look at the idiot, he
can barely close his thighs, who cares if those
people die. A manhole in Bucharest today
exploded, the Nikkei just imploded, it's a great
time to make a killing in gold. You must burn it
to stay alive, get off my land you'll get fried, turn
to me, I'll be your guide, I alone can fix it.

The heat is coming, no one can fix it, no one can
stop the ships yet vacationers watch
them sink eating fish and chips. What a drag
on their view! So much death in the way of their due,
I want to see clear blue seas, not you! Get out of
my way, I'm closing the doors shutting the window
cranking the thermostat to blue, now you won't see
me and I can't see you.

# Windward

Listen to what the air
is saying tonight

my friend, you've
been ashore a long

while, the time
for your sail

to fill is here.
We're standing on

the verge with you,
take our arms

we'll lift you into
this boat

you've been building
your whole life:

the beam-ends are
lined with your labor,

the arc of visibility
is clear,

everything that ever
was awaits you at sea.

Tell it to us when
we arrive

in due time, in ships
you taught us to sail.

# Yard Dogs

It was a town where dogs chased
anything that moved. Bikes, cars,
you. People left their gates open
a crack. The dogs knew to wait
until you were upon them before
exploding into carols of snarl.
Frothing, raging, this-chain-isn't-
going-to-stop-me spasms that'd
end abruptly when you hightailed
it around a corner, ass forward,
legs pinwheeling, the dog behind
you doing whatever it is dogs do
when they laugh to themselves.

# Dream

Remember when we had bodies

and we felt like hollow-boned

animals of wind?     Now all this

touching without touching, as if

this screen     ever made the under-

side of a leaf go silver. Tell me

a story and make it count. Turn

me back into something grand.

I want a plume of bold pattern. Let me

dive at great speeds. I don't want

to murder, I want to love the air.

# Burning the Days

I was fire then everything
burned   the days   the hours

quickened each night as darkness
came thermal belts and fine smoke

led us out to scorch the dark
the next day our work

under a canopy of clouds
swinging our arms like lanterns

happy and unaware walking fast
in columns of air

# Sailing

A bone-white gull slides as

if it's wearing socks on hardwood

floors back & forth in the air

passing my window like Tom Cruise

in that movie. Streets deserted

but it doesn't stop, eyes wild & yellow

with what—happiness?

Does a bird feel joy? Does it need to

be seen feeling . . . to feel? Maybe

when wind expands & contracts

like breath inside the landbound

the word means something different

to be able to rest on it

lie down upon it     climb it

fall through it & then catch

a rung—*there*

that it's feeling without skin to hold it in

maybe simply becoming a sail for joy

blown wildly across the world

or down the avenues.

# Quarantine

One night, lowering the blinds,
I saw a couple across the way

playing cards at their dinner table.
They'd laid a felt mat across

the wood: he was dealing, she arranging
her hand. From across the street

I could see her smile, or maybe imagined
it. He was talking—maybe taunting

her. Come here, I said, look at
this couple—and you said

I see them most nights. They
eat dinner and then move over

and play. They laugh
and laugh. They're laughing

right now, I pointed out, then you reached
up and stroked my back.

# Airless

Nothing. Not a thing, not a drip nor a skerrick of air
pipped through my tiny slot. Just puff and wheeze,

eyeballs fixed on the gurgling humidifier
belching menthol-flavored cubits of

breath into my room, into my tattered lungs,
serenading my struggle

in blue-fugue loneliness, everyone
elsewhere. Everyone having fun. How many

hours I spent this way as a child, I don't know.
A thousand? More? I lived in a town of

tornadoes and blizzards, during the heyday
of the bomb. Sipping on air that ran out felt

like practice, my night watch, protection
from the feeling of ever having protection.

# Trees

# Shipbuilding

The line stretched for a kilometer
three thousand people trembling

in the cold, rain turning to sleet,
to bid farewell to a library.

An army of children had emptied the shelves,
carted books across town like the dead

who'd once erupted from the graves of Paris,
whose skeletons were hauled by horse

and hand to the catacombs
where they'd rest for eternity.

Now Oslo's books will overlook the sea,
readers will mark time by how they

recall when a library was a landlocked
fortress, a bunker of cement and paper,

the only ocean the one you saw in
*Moby-Dick* or Rachel Carson.

Teaching us to say goodbye was how
we remembered what once lived:

to acknowledge the destruction
committed in plain air.

What if we said goodbye more often
the way children do

when they first learn how,
every parting momentous—

like a ship leaving port, the weather
deck full of people searching for

beloveds, to wave goodbye and good
luck, as if luck might stop a gust

from tearing a ship off course.

We look fondly on the days when
we stood the sea different from the sea

because one we'd seen and the other
we'd seen in our mind's eye, a way

of saying we are learning to live in a world
where imagination and remembrance are the same thing

because they allow us to deny that so
much left behind worked perfectly fine.

# Singing

In Arabic it means wood, and in its cousin
Syriac, burning wood. Cognate to *od*, as in
the old Hebrew, stick used to stir wood
in a fire. Some days it burns, on others
it simply is, and on occasion it stirs what's
there. Today from the bedroom the oud's sound
wakes me and the body inside my body turns over,
the one that remembers not being yours, merely
a visitor, I'd never heard Wadih el-Safi sing
his mawals, a longing unashamed. I'd find you
in the kitchen cooking your father's food,
air smoky and fragrant, sharpened by
lament. I'd never imagine how cinder-lined
were your days, how little of what was
remained, I'd grown up in a country of
thin wood, pale sky, dateless palms, but you
welcomed me anyway, and as Wadih el-Safi
belted out his psalms, you did me
the kindness of promising me this wasn't
practice for what time would bring.

# The Language of Trees

How little a tree says.
What is a canopy but an offer of
shelter? A branch but a

search for light? What is a trunk
but a commitment?

Or bark but an awareness
that life eventually burns? That neighbors

are prone to attack, to latch on,
to harvest the finest inner

essence they can reach
by pincer, by fungus,

by ax. Trees have learned
these things over time.

How to offer up the dead parts
of their bodies first

so the world we call the world
will ignore that most of what

matters happens out of sight
a few feet beneath

our boots, where they pass
the cup and needn't call

it generosity, or spread
news of a coming drought,

draw water to a dying friend
because maybe

there's no single
word for tree, or perhaps

that's all there has been—
alarm—for some time.

The tree listeners say so,
those magical few who

decode the electrical
pulses that travel deep

in the root structures
that fan out like galaxies

ganglia mixing with fungi
a crowded bazaar

of trade, friendship,
even love that stretches

for miles tells stories an epic
of love and despair.

What the scientists
hear, they mostly

say, is panic and distress,
though trees

might be saying other things
they don't know how

to hear yet from the
hormones that course

through their giant
collective body,

as if any of us do not
feel a similar planing down

to what is sayable when
so much is

ringing in our limbs,
rising up in the low frequencies,

the rush
of familiarity

a copse
in the woods

huddling together in the wind,
a spell

asking for confirmation

as if what needs to be said
needs to be said.

# Wood

One morning time trips a reel
and I'm confronted with
the object I will become
carpentered for eternity.
Here the wood's grain
the carve and gouge
that felt like time
but was merely my body.
How little it belongs
to me even the face
I've inherited from a hundred
mothers and fathers.
The grove beneath
vast and humble waits
her arms so huge
she has built a house for
billions and has word left
over for bookshelves, pews,
for tools and decoration.

# Among the Trees

Each morning on the common Martha stops
beneath the conifers, paws on dry needles,
the part of our daily stroll where

she allows me to kiss her stilled German
head. A long way from boar hunts and pheasant
shoots she was bred for in 1840s Saxony.

The spruce are emigrants too. The copse
planted to temper winds on the newly
cleared wood. Now they stand

apart, transplants like all souls turned
toward one another, while we pass
through, a softer wind.

# Still

Every day at lunch the gray heron
canters down from her branch in the brook

leaving behind turquoise eggs. There were
two birds, but kids killed one with a slingshot, so

now she hooks alone, casting with her giant
beak. Stirring the water with a foot. The legends

tell of what revenge nature will wreak, we'll
be torn limb from limb, they'll feast on our necks.

None of this seems true of the heron in the
brook, using her wings to create shade, lure

small fish into the coves made by trash
visitors dump amidst the glades. Cans of Coke,

T-shirts, a dishwasher, an old skirt. It's become
the breakfast table for her. And us, what are we for?

To watch, mourn, to exclaim gladly?
I've nothing to hunt, to trap, nothing

to own, walking these woods with a fading
map, miles from my suburban home.

The heron looks up, and seeing I am neither
prey nor threat, returns to her disguise,

vanishes again in the weeds, standing so still she
is simply a reed, a white bill, two eyes.

# Show

At sundown kestrels call to each other across the gar-
den, flocking in the large elm tree that stands over the
shed like an elder waiting patiently at a parade. In a year
they'll disperse, as some hunters must, but now they
take a slow route home, crisscrossing the air in forma-
tion like pilots doing barrel rolls, loop the loops, even
hammerheads. All to cascades of song. When the singing
stops and the birds still, the trees move gently in the wet
air like applause.

## The Secret Country

Before they go the way of Checker cabs,
rotary phones, cassette tapes, or bootjacks,
let's remember that riding to work on the upper deck
of a London bus as it brushed the skirted canopy
of trees in late spring was like stepping
into the green-lit rooms of shade and wonder
we'd been promised as children, a scratch
of branches along its red roof, the whoosh
of leaves music to a den we need to move
past to see we've been living in it all along.

# Borrowed Finery

And on those nights ice beveling the windows
Leslie and I would visit Patricia in her flat

glowing lamps and radiator heat
Philadelphia winter whipping with its usual

rages as we drank mail-order coffee
thought to smell of Paris

whiffs of chocolate and cinnamon how you think
Paris smells when you haven't been there

my mother never went she drank the same
coffee cupped her mug like Patricia warmed

with that same Scotch-Irish blush
Vivaldi burbling in the background

like a Saint-Germain bistro
an imagined city encouraging us there in real

ways on the outskirts of Philadelphia
comfort important even when it came from a box

how starkly good our lives seem to me now
planed to an ascetic purity of study

I worked then as an art model waking in
Leslie's bed we'd walk to class

together and then I'd disrobe
my body still warm from her

in that instant it became something
outside me—for an hour I sat in the gap

between me and the form I was born into
not looking out simply resting

the best pose reading Woolf's diaries
*a wet day and I am glad of the rain*

*I have talked too much*
what joy not to speak to simply exist

the scratching a music of concentration
the furl and crack of a new

sheet being turned even in frustration
a beautiful sound its own weather

space heater warming behind me like a
very focused sunbeam

all day afterward I'd feel the palm of it
on my backside until the chill set in

——

Thirty years ago those visits I open the bare
cupboard this morning in New York radiators

hissing windows smeared with snow
and there's but one packet of coffee a leftover gift

from the same mail-order company
still sending out coffee with classical music

dreams of Paris and all my bodies sit inside
my body some of them still asking for cinnamon

some asking for her and some no longer asking
a city so quiet it's almost imaginary

the past an unlit street
I can follow home in the dark

# Icicle

Even water
changes its
mind mid-
drip from
the bearded
skull of a
streetlamp
strange to
be given
proof sound
comes from
movement
and noise
chaos—I
am the still-
fumed center
of the world
holding its
breath on a
burned thing
cooled

## Centuries in the Woods

When I lived in the woods I began to hear
conversations that had unfolded
across centuries. Chats, debates, gossips
so long the porch upon which they'd been
whispered surely had been replaced
several times. I often stopped walking
to listen. Deep in the woodland,
ground mossy and sopping from late August
rain, the air rippled with greenish light.
Sometimes there was birdsong,
but in early afternoon they'd be silent, as even
the raptors tucked into hollows or slept
amidst the spray of branches. They'd stopped
flush-cutting these trees decades ago so
the air crackled like a pub past closing time
when every story deserves a telling
and the voices are loud and full
of music and the horizon has grown
blue-black with tomorrow's morning.

# Exile

You can tell by the walls
whoever lives here doesn't
want to be seen. Thieves
know when to leave,
brick by brick they take
apart castles and rebuild
them elsewhere, in Rio,
in sunny Seychelles,
along the Dalmatian coast,
they buy up ancient flats
in Paris and Rome,
Buenos Aires and
here, in a leafy Outer
London village once given
to Hugh de Neville by
the king. Birthplace
of John Galsworthy—surely
he knew an exile or two,
in need of safety for the few.
Now if you want a walled compound
for twenty thousand a month it's
your borough of choice. Saddam
Hussein's daughter owned
a bungalow along Golf Club
Drive once. Did her father
ever drop in? Did the family
saunter into the Iraqi food
store, where refugees
and their onetime
persecutors shop side
by side? Or maybe
the ex–party heads don't *shop*,

just as it wasn't their fingers
rivering millions through
Swiss accounts and keypad-
access private banks.
Amazing, how finely tuned the
ears of real power are to
the winds of danger.
The bags, when grabbed,
have been packed a long time,
then the so-called looting begins—
on the evening news:
statues, empty palaces.
As if the fixtures are
worth anything. As if the real
wealth hasn't already been
lifted and stashed long ago where it has been
for centuries: right in the open
at the empire's center.

# The Trees of City Hall

There are 5.2 million in
New York City, many
of them London plane trees
making grand alleys with their
hearty trunks, also Norway maples,
throwing shade like a
Scandinavian hangover. A tulip
tree in Queens dates back
450 years, while another in Staten
Island, barely middle-aged at 300,
stands almost as tall. They call
it the Colossus. Imagine if they'd
been free to grow. In early America
tulips were chopped down for canoes
and paper, used for musical instruments.
How many school kids have learned cello
on one? Some other giants remain
around City Hall in the park
born in the 1600s as the town
commons. Protests against the Stamp
Act began in this square; in 1776
New Yorkers came to hear George Washington
read the Declaration of Independence.
When slavery was abolished in 1827
the celebration lasted two days. Riots,
yellow fever, speeches by Boss Tweed, pleas
of the hungry during the Great Depression
and last week. All of it heard by the trees
that stand around City Hall like a group of
elders on a Friday night when wind
is cold, rubbing their hands together.
They easily outdate the building,

finished in 1812, and city government,
not to mention the police force, dissolved in
1857, leading to a riot, and the
new department modeled on
London's own metropolitan police,
brought in like the plane tree to
temper a city on the brink. Now the
descendants of those changes,
New York City's ubiquitous blue
wall, stand about, backs to the street,
flicking through their phones, barked in
heavy armor. How long will
they last? Meanwhile the trees loom
overhead—as they have since whale
fat powered streetlamps—inhaling
the latest storm to be weathered, piping
out clean air, even here.

# Windbreak

In hurricane season the old trees
suffer. Especially the ones
standing alone. Their roots no
match for a summer wind
churning at sea, inhaling slights
and salt air, then rushing

to shore flicking buses and restaurants
aside, erasing the past. One hard gust
and they're gone. In groups
live oaks can survive, even at 130 m.p.h.
So will buttonwoods, otherwise known as
American sycamores, which will grow huge

with deep soil and a few neighbors.
But these days to be sturdy is to bend.
So the dogwood and jelly palm,
the pygmy date and crape myrtle,
hardy limestone shrubs, boxleaf stopper,
they don't ask for much

are happy to guard a house, form a
windbreak, while one newscaster after another
exits their blacked-out SUVs in slickers
to stand in driving rain to prove
their heroism as they give us more time,
more time.

# Dusk

*for Barry Lopez*

Horizon turns from blue to black
with infinite tenderness in London
tonight. Yet even at full dusk a smear
of cobalt rings the tree line. Maybe
endless love awaits us. I know you believed
so, even as forests and rivers turned to fire,
libraries to ash. Now that you're not here
to tend them, the lamps you lit remain for us.
Sometimes it's important to see the darkness,
you would say, to regard one another,
and our trembling. Or on other nights, like
now: we must look up. How is this same
moon in my sky hanging over Eugene these
small hours? Do you feel its comforts?
As you sleep through this final stretch
how badly I want you to know we have
the torches now, my friend, we'll protect the flame,
you are free to be the wind again.

# Colors

Thirty miles south of Dallas the air smells of ozone and water. Thunderheads on the horizon in shades of indigo. It's a fifty-five-mile drive, we'll be there in an hour. I wonder how these colors looked to the Kickapoo back then, to the wranglers and oil prospectors who'd suck two hundred million barrels of oil from this county, paying for wide-plank porches and soaring ceilings in mansions passed father to son, then to no one. Granite town halls built to last half a millennium. Kitchens pharmacy white, whiter than white, a drop of cream will mark the wainscoting or the weave of thread in linen drying on a clothesline—white against the green pines, green against the battered-tin sky, where buds turn so fragrantly open it's hard to imagine the world is sick.

I arrive in a town called Corsicana. Named after a Texas patriot's father's home island in the Mediterranean, Corsica. Many of the homes were built when some farm kids were sewn into their clothes at first frost, then not cut out until spring. What did white look like to them? Did it haunt them, did it taste like that long winter fug? Did it make them think of twisters or other monsters of wind touching down and scooping up animals and precious clay and barns, anything that wasn't nailed to the earth? None of us are, when we think of it—we're all just barely touching ground: a piece of cotton stuck in a bush. A simple gust could carry most of us away. A puff of a storm's half-breathed breath.

Maybe this is what I see in the brow of a woman standing in the back row of a women's league group portrait, Corsicana, 1894. The sense of worry: none of her world was safe, none of it was made to last, even if the buildings couldn't be budged with a locomotive. Pewter and gray; polished potbelly; base of an old bois d'arc; the nobility of limestone shot through with white; all the colors of her world more stable than her world. Richer, deeper. What did she see when, nights noisy with insects, she closed her eyes? Or in winter—the breath in her throat full of iron and wool? Blue comes first on the cool spectrum, especially below freezing. Had a trick of light ever turned the air around Chambers Creek turquoise? Was the air about a lover once glowing like bluebonnets? Did she ever see a red jacket worn against an inky sky? What sort of stain would that make on memory? In her short life?

In her day, for this woman in this portrait, her brow furrowed without a line, her eyes etched by concern, for her, pharmacies would have traveled by horse and wagon, clinking with bottles the color of honey holding powders the shade of pecan and buffalo grass. Stirred into well water, tasting of tin, they became elixirs. Transformative potions. Did she feel she was making herself anew when she drank them? Like when months after a tailor stuck a dress onto a mannequin in Paris, its design might appear in an issue of *Mme. Demorest's Mirror of Fashion*, the kind of magazine an enterprising beautician in a Texas town might put on oak end tables for customers who wanted to touch the clean glass mirror of self-creation.

What would that pharmacy look like, if it wasn't a magazine but a tiny glowing little miniature apothecary you could rest on the edge of your bed? You could plug it in and keep it on all night. Light candles inside it. A little diorama, all to scale, full of tiny, bearded potion-sellers and golden bottles and pollen jars. Would it keep the darkness at bay? Make it possible to live under skies as awesome and frightening as the ones this woman might have faced? Would it have saved her worry, such a pharmacy? Or made of it—her fear—something she could roll in her palm each night until her hand tired of the motion, and at last she slept? Or until the blue light of dawn, light so thin it's almost white, began to creep up the wall, and she rose to make coffee?

The Latin word *curitas* means cherish, not cure. Here's what colors are telling us—what we want to cure ourselves of, or at least tame, is what we need to see more clearly. Siberian squill with its steel-blue pollen, creosote leaves and their hidden water. Sloping blacklands and mile after mile of mesquite. All of it continues and persists and then dies. This in a color-starved part of the world. Maybe that's what she was looking at, this woman, trapped forever in 1894, squinting not out at a world of worry, but perhaps at a world printed on the back of her eye, one full of colors. Maybe she was wondering when it would be that they would exist outside her head, when they'd be painted onto a body, or the sides of buildings, or the face you see around a face when you take it all in.

# Receiving

Three things
will get her
to drop the ball:
a crap, a fox,
a ripe blackberry.
Normally she
crashes into
brambles like
a rugby player in open
field. This morning
the sun emerges.
She places her ball
on the grass,
approaches the bush
tenderly, her wide
snout sniffing, searching,
until it finds
one perfect berry,
which she accepts
like a gift only she
could sense
was being offered.

# Without

Maybe one day I will learn how to live
without, without her and her, and she and
them, without him. Lately, I am mostly
absence. I have lived so long within
my body's clever disguise, so complete
this heart, these eyes. But maybe a body's

largely past tense. Like a house empty but
for hours a chill blows through it. Maybe
I am like wind briefly still, a column
of air that found a form to fill. Waiting
for a sign to go where wind goes when it's
not with us—when without becomes within.

# The Green Tram

In my forty-sixth year there
are so many things
I want to tell you.
How everyone is
drunk at Wimbledon,
and a fox has come to live in our
garden. We feed
him duck livers from a can.
In return he doesn't destroy
the plantings. We are shunned
on the block.

      Oh, there are days when
the darkness falls
too fast and I feel myself
spinning. And the tram
that runs past the windbreak
beyond the house—so snug
and cozy as we approach winter—
it glides by with a terrifying
gentleness.

      Aglow.
A few passengers inside
decked in masks. Bent
into newspapers
as in prayer. A sigh
of wind and they become a winking
light receding through the trees.
I wonder if I will ever understand your
inability to answer me

in these thoughts where
you live. You inside my life
a green-lit perfection, so loving
and yet so soundless I can almost
address you. I think of
you every morning
as I spread marmalade
on my toast in this strange
country a decade later.

# Fables

Mornings on the lake
I woke in dawn's green
glove, air soft with water,
narrow bed still warm,
she'd sit, light as a coverlet
on the mattress, tell me
of a lonely bird
who circled the lake's blue
stripe, looking down on
its shale beaches and
frosted wavelets, the
halo of beech trees
that stood around it
like a circle in prayer
saying to all the boys climbing
from sleep's cove:
Come greet the world anew.
Forty years later, along a fjord
clouded by sea smoke, the white
bird glides by again, the air soft
now with water,
the hills greened by mist,
this narrow bed still warm with sleep,
and I, I imagine its eye peering down,
all the way down to the boys
who are no longer boys,
saying Begin, begin again.

# The Red Umbrella

It rains all morning
in Frogner Park

a sheet of green fog

crowds orbit Vigeland's
granite figures

like dancers in a merry-go-round

bodies slick as wet marble
leaning into one another

raising each other up
like torches

trying to remember
this is what a

body can be

the pile of a family
a thrash of lovers

an angry weeping
boy

naked and alone

in the center a monolith
the figures

collide and try to come
together as if all

our pain comes
from our apartness

A lone woman

under a red umbrella
watches the figures

like they are a show

the great lawn breathes heat
into January air

*we have more than enough* you said
and in that instant

I knew it had always been true
we have made this religion

of turning skyward to say thanks
as if you weren't

right here next to me and love
the red umbrella

# Voices

Late at night in the house by the woods
I hear kids walking home from the tram
their voices as faint
as the beginnings of rain
they draw near and there are words
*yes, fourteen or fifteen,*
*I know, definitely fifteen*
boys speaking to one another
while conversations run around and
beneath them like underground streams
At their age we drove everywhere in cars
our voices floating free of our bodies
out open windows the way sky lanterns
will rise of their own burning
making similar notations of tally
the car's motor our track times days until summer break
we yearned to measure everything
pin it to the earth as we floated through

The streetlamp throws a pale white glow into the bedroom
nights we've spent in this bed awake breathing in each
other's dreams waiting for the phone to ring in last days
when talk stops and deep silence has opened up
as far away someone we love enters that most private moment
the ultimate final solitude a wood so deep a voice cannot
depart and yet we huddle round ask for words
and sound and acknowledgment
when what the voices are becoming is a sound
beyond sound one near when far and forever

I remember hearing it her voice after she died so close
like she was there on the bed the way when I was small

she would lie next to me speak softly into my ear
what trick of evolution gave us this ability to soothe ourselves
with the sound of our departed there is no such thing
as a swan song when one dies its other half simply goes

briefly silent Now the kids' voices are so near as
if they are walking through the room
I sit up to greet them, leaving the bed
to stand by the window and mark their arrival
in that brief slip of time they've passed by
the front of the house and have become a shadow
of bodies departing the gray-green dark
voices softer and softer it's as if
they have never been here at all

# Acknowledgments

"Borrowed Finery" appeared online in *The Common*.

"Dusk" appeared on the *Orion Magazine* website as part of a memorial to Barry Lopez.

"Friendship" ran in *Alta Journal*.

"Icicle" appeared in *Michigan Quarterly Review*.

"Loneliness" appeared in *The Common*.

"Quarantine" was included in *Together in a Sudden Strangeness: America's Poets Respond to the Pandemic*, edited by Alice Quinn.

"Shipbuilding" ran in *Klassekampen* in Nynorsk.

"Still" appeared in *Orion Magazine*.

Grateful acknowledgment to the editors involved in these publications, and special thanks to Michael Wiegers, for edits too metaphysical to call mere edits.

## About the Author

John Freeman is the founder of *Freeman's*, the literary annual of new writing, and an executive editor at Alfred A. Knopf. His work includes the poetry collections *Maps* and *The Park*, the book-length essay *Dictionary of the Undoing*, and several anthologies, among them *Tales of Two Americas*, a volume on inequality in America, *Tales of Two Planets*, which examines the climate crisis globally, and *There's a Revolution Outside, My Love*, coedited by Tracy K. Smith, a portrait of the United States on the cusp of revolution, climate crisis, and the upheavals of a pandemic. His work has been translated into over twenty languages, and his poems have appeared in *The New Yorker*, *The Paris Review*, and *ZYZZYVA*. The former editor of *Granta*, he teaches at NYU and hosts the California Book Club, a monthly discussion of a book from California for *Alta Journal*.

Poetry is vital to language and living. Since 1972, Copper Canyon Press has published extraordinary poetry from around the world to engage the imaginations and intellects of readers, writers, booksellers, librarians, teachers, students, and donors.

COPPER CANYON PRESS WISHES TO EXTEND A SPECIAL THANKS TO THE FOLLOW-
ING SUPPORTERS WHO PROVIDED FUNDING DURING THE COVID-19 PANDEMIC:

4Culture
Academy of American Poets (Literary Relief Fund)
City of Seattle Office of Arts & Culture
Community of Literary Magazines and Presses (Literary Relief Fund)
Economic Development Council of Jefferson County
National Book Foundation (Literary Relief Fund)
Poetry Foundation
U.S. Department of the Treasury Payroll Protection Program

WE ARE GRATEFUL FOR THE MAJOR SUPPORT PROVIDED BY:

THE PAUL G. ALLEN
FAMILY FOUNDATION

TO LEARN MORE ABOUT UNDERWRITING
COPPER CANYON PRESS TITLES,
PLEASE CALL 360-385-4925 EXT. 103

## WE ARE GRATEFUL FOR THE MAJOR SUPPORT PROVIDED BY:

Richard Andrews

Anonymous (3)

Jill Baker and Jeffrey Bishop

Anne and Geoffrey Barker

In honor of Ida Bauer, Betsy
Gifford, and Beverly Sachar

Donna Bellew

Matthew Bellew

Sarah Bird

Will Blythe

John Branch

Diana Broze

John R. Cahill

Sarah Cavanaugh

Stephanie Ellis-Smith and
Douglas Smith

Austin Evans

Saramel Evans

Mimi Gardner Gates

Gull Industries Inc. on behalf of
William True

The Trust of Warren A. Gummow

William R. Hearst III

Carolyn and Robert Hedin

David and Jane Hibbard

Bruce Kahn

Phil Kovacevich and Eric Wechsler

Lakeside Industries Inc. on behalf
of Jeanne Marie Lee

Maureen Lee and Mark Busto

Peter Lewis and Johnna Turiano

Ellie Mathews and Carl Youngmann
as The North Press

Larry Mawby and Lois Bahle

Hank and Liesel Meijer

Jack Nicholson

Gregg Orr

Petunia Charitable Fund and
adviser Elizabeth Hebert

Suzanne Rapp and Mark Hamilton

Adam and Lynn Rauch

Emily and Dan Raymond

Joseph C. Roberts

Jill and Bill Ruckelshaus

Cynthia Sears

Kim and Jeff Seely

Joan F. Woods

Barbara and Charles Wright

In honor of C.D. Wright,
from Forrest Gander

Caleb Young as C. Young Creative

The dedicated interns and
faithful volunteers of
Copper Canyon Press

The Chinese character for poetry is made up
of two parts: "word" and "temple."
It also serves as pressmark for
Copper Canyon Press.

This book is set in Verdigris MVB Pro.
Book design by Gopa & Ted2, Inc.
Printed on archival-quality paper.